Usborne First Experiences
The New Baby

Anne Civardi

Illustrated by Stephen Cartwright

Edited by Michelle Bates
Cover design by Neil Francis

There is a little yellow duck hiding on every double page. Can you find it?

This is the Bunn family.

Mr. Bunn

Mrs. Bunn

Lucy Bunn

Spock

Tom Bunn

Bertie

Lucy is five and Tom is three. Mrs. Bunn is going to have a baby soon.

Granny and Grandpa come to stay.

They are going to look after Lucy and Tom when Mrs. Bunn is in the hospital. Lucy and Tom are excited to see them.

The Bunns get ready for the new baby.

There is a lot to do before the baby is born. Mr. and Mrs. Bunn decorate the baby's bedroom.

Lucy and Tom help too. Mrs. Bunn paints the bed for the
baby to sleep in. Lucy uses the baby's bath to wash her doll.

Mrs. Bunn feels the baby coming.

Mrs. Bunn wakes up in the middle of the night. She thinks that the baby will be born very soon.

Everyone wakes up.

Mr. Bunn gets ready to take her to the hospital while Grandpa phones to say that they are on their way.

The baby is born.

It is a little girl. Mr. and Mrs. Bunn are very happy. They are going to name her Susie.

Nurse Cherry weighs Susie to see how heavy she is, and measures her to see how long she is.

Susie is wrapped in a blanket. She has a name tag on her tiny wrist so she doesn't get mixed up with other babies.

As soon as Dad gets home, he tells Lucy and Tom all about their baby sister, Susie. They can't wait to see her.

They visit Susie.

The next day, Mr. Bunn takes Lucy and Tom to the hospital. They are very excited to see their mother and baby sister.

Mrs. Bunn is in a room with two other mothers. They have new babies too. One of the mothers has twins.

The next day, Mrs. Bunn and Susie come home.

Mr. Bunn picks them up from the hospital. Everyone is excited and wants to hold the baby.

Susie goes to bed.

Susie is very sleepy. Mrs. Bunn is tired too. She will need a lot of help from Lucy, Tom and Mr. Bunn.

Mrs. Bunn feeds Susie.

When Susie is hungry, Mrs. Bunn feeds her with milk. Susie will need to be fed many times each day.

Susie has a bath.

Now it is time for Susie's bath. Mr. Bunn is very careful.
Lucy helps her Dad wash and dry Susie.

The Bunn family goes out.

Mr. and Mrs. Bunn, Lucy and Tom take Susie for a walk.
They are all very excited about the new baby.

This edition published in 2005 by Usborne Publishing Ltd, Usborne House, 83-85 Saffron Hill, London EC1N 8RT, England.
Copyright © 2005, 1992 Usborne Publishing Ltd.
First published in America in 2005. UE
The name Usborne and the devices ⚌ ⊕ are Trade Marks of Usborne Publishing Ltd.